MOTHERS
AND OTHER PEOPLE

poems by

Karen Taylor

Finishing Line Press
Georgetown, Kentucky

MOTHERS
AND OTHER PEOPLE

Copyright © 2024 by Karen Taylor
ISBN 979-8-88838-689-7 First Edition
All rights reserved under International and Pan-American Copyright Conventions. No part of this book may be reproduced in any manner whatsoever without written permission from the publisher, except in the case of brief quotations embodied in critical articles and reviews.

ACKNOWLEDGMENTS

Special thanks to Lesléa Newman for her coaching, and to my wife Laura Antoniou for her unwavering support.

"Dressing The Body" was originally published February 2024 in Ghost Light Lit's Issue 1: Grief Machine.

Publisher: Leah Huete de Maines
Editor: Christen Kincaid
Cover Art: Nancy Nicodemus
Author Photo: Karen Taylor
Cover Design: Elizabeth Maines McCleavy

Order online: www.finishinglinepress.com
also available on amazon.com

Author inquiries and mail orders:
Finishing Line Press
PO Box 1626
Georgetown, Kentucky 40324
USA

Contents

Too Late 1

Michael, row the boat ashore, hallelujah 2

Hometown Tulips 4

Insomnia 6

The Grown-Ups Table 7

I'll be seeing you 10

Untying Family Ties 11

4AM Toledo 14

After The Stroke 16

Homesick 17

Belated 18

Memory 19

To The Corner and Back 20

11PM Shopping List 21

What to Put in the Obituary 23

Unmothered 25

The Last Jew Standing 27

Dressing The Body 29

Passover 2022 30

ephemera 32

Dedicated to Nancy Nicodemus (December 4, 1934-December 2, 2023): poet, professor, adventurer, and my mother.

Too Late

Is it ever too late to start over?

it may be too late to begin at the beginning
it's too far gone to remember how it all began,
and way too late to pretend it never happened

it is too late to take back the words,
to call,
to bite one's tongue
even if the blood flows freely
to mend old wounds

they say that it is never too late
to ask for forgiveness
and never too late to forgive
but is it too late to receive forgiveness
when it is offered

and what if forgiveness comes late?
does my forgiveness matter only to me?
does it matter if it only matters to me
that I've forgiven you?

Michael, row the boat ashore, hallelujah

my earliest memory
is a song
my mother humming
her voice vibrating
through her chest
against my cheek.

She rocked me
in a pine-scented chair
the floorboard squeaking
when the curved wood
pressed forward
then back
she sang softly
green pastures
on the other side
my eyes blinking
more and more slowly
as I drifted to sleep

she sang,
almost whispering
her breath
brushing my hair
she rocked me
the dark wood cool
when I was feverish
and blistered from pox

or teary and frightened
from a slammed door
and shouting
that jerked me awake.
A nightmare,
my mother whispered
as I traced the thin groove
on the chair's arm

with a trembling finger
The river is deep
The river is wide

I clambered into
that smooth low seat
before I could walk,
grabbed the thin round rails
the curves the shape
of my mother's back
pulled myself up and over.
I rocked all by myself,
one foot pushing
off the floor
reading, for hours
humming under my breath

I took that chair with me
when I moved out,
polished its spindles
settled it in a corner
near a window
so I could rock
myself to sleep
milk and honey
on the other side
Hallelujah

Hometown Tulips

The tulips bloom
in the colors of a toddler's paintbox;
filling photo albums in my mother's house.
my childhood of tulips.

That's me, captured by Kodak
in a yellow and brown plaid jumper,
rounded white Peter Pan collar,
chubby fist around a bright green stem
bending a pink tulip to my nose.

There I am again
next to a miniature windmill
squinting at the sun
acres of tulips stretching behind me
a Mondrian painting of yellows, reds, orange, and indigo
white shorts and knee socks marred by dirt.

Me and my best friend
mug for the camera
in Dutch costumes sewn by her mother
tulips the color of sunshine and peaches
or cool purples with lavender highlights
we grow taller on each page.

A blurry photo taken from the sidewalk
as a band marches through town,
a Tulip Time parade
vibrant flowers planted between sidewalk and curb
our faces are out of focus; but I'm certain
I'm sweating in my red-trimmed wool uniform.

Standing in the front yard
white graduation robe
mortarboard and gold tassel dangling
a border of fuschia tulips with white frilled edges

hide my shoes
glassy smile
hides my thoughts.

Insomnia

"Let's take a walk" she suggests
at one in the morning, when I can't sleep.

We stroll around the block
slippers scuffing the grit at the edge of the asphalt,
lake breezes sneaking under our nightgowns,
quiet voices mingling with the cicadas and frogs.

I lay awake now, and wonder:
What did we talk about, on those walks?
And why was my mother always awake
staring out the window
sitting in the dark?

The Grown-Ups Table

My grandmother's oak dining room table
magically expands for holidays.
Matching carved chairs
appear from parts unknown
lace-trimmed table cloth is ironed
matching linen napkins pressed
then set with bridal rose china
pulled from the hutch
for Grandpa and Grandma
two aunts, two uncles
my parents.

In the next room
my brother
five cousins, and me
tilt precariously
on folding chairs
dragged in from the garage.
Knees knock against
rickety card tables
elbows bump, spill
milk-filled Dixie cups
soak folded paper towels.
We pass potatoes
toss dinner rolls
stifle giggles,
ignore the grownups.

My oldest cousin
arrives one year
in a brown suit
once worn by his father.
He brings a girl
in a green and gold dress
and a diamond ring
once worn by my grandmother.

Two more chairs
are added
to the grown-ups table.

The six of us
left at the card tables
roll our eyes, shrug,
fill our Chinet disposables,
dig elbows into each others' ribs,
count ourselves lucky
to be at the fun table.

The oak table expands
conjures a longer tablecloth
and two more matching chairs.
A younger cousin
with a shiny new husband
parade through,
ignore our dented card table
where, single, I sit
with her single, older sister.

My grandfather dies.
Our first Thanksgiving
without him
married cousins drag
another card table,
and more folding chairs
from the garage
for toddlers,
then return
to the oak table
leaving us
babysitting
our first cousins
once removed.

My brother
brings his lover
a handsome man.
Year after year
we sit together
with our oldest single cousin
at the card table
sharing wry smiles
over soiled paper plates
our Dixie cups
filled now with wine.

I'll be seeing you

in all the old familiar places
my mother hums
and perhaps, when she hums she hears her mother,

or maybe it's Jo Stafford, on the radio
through the doors of the American Legion Hall
where her father tended bar on weekends
for soldiers coming back home
to dance with their sweethearts

like my aunt, cheek resting against the chest
of her high school sweetheart.
They wrote to each other every day, my mother told me
when he was in the service.

Perhaps it was the letters that transformed
my uncle's uniform from soldier to letter carrier,
driving the arrow-straight county roads
cornfields on one side, soybeans on the other,
mile after mile after mile.

From above, they look like a patchwork quilt
neat squares that align through my window
as I fly from the coast to the center

where my mother, the last of her siblings
sits on her porch
humming.

Untying Family Ties

The corner drug store (Rexall)
has a soda fountain
I set my suitcase under the stool
order my last hand pumped cherry cola.
Some summers, it was a Green River
or sass'parilla
poured over crushed ice
shared with siblings and cousins
now scattered to other places

The soda jerk/pharmacist
tilts his head, asks my name
I tell him mine and my grandmother's.
He snaps a bony finger,
places me in his world.
I'm Ruth's Nancy's daughter
he remembers
my grandmother's wedding
how proud she was when my mother
went to college
he tosses me a denture-filled grin
tells me his granddaughter is also in college
studying to be a doctor
adds a scoop of vanilla ice cream
to my glass.

I walk past the American Legion Hall (Post 215)
second home for the men of my family
uncles, brothers, cousins
and my grandfather, designated barman
pouring foaming beer
from a newly tapped keg
for the Fire Department volunteers
or the Friday Fish Fry
ladies welcome as guests
or members of the Auxiliary

Ladies don't drink
as a rule
and certainly not beer
but perhaps
a sloe gin and Pepsi
for special occasions
like my cousin's wedding reception
where I danced in heels
and had my first grown up drink
both for the first time.
I sit on the bench, etched with family names
fallen in the Great Wars
switch out my shoes
and leave the heels behind.

The Post Office (46761)
boasts a WPA mural I never noticed before:
"The Corn School." A village festival
surrounding the red brick courthouse.
I've been to Corn School
my cousins, my mother, my aunts
my grandmother and her sisters
marched in Corn School Parades
were crowned Corn School Queens
entered preserves and pies in Corn School contests
ate deep-fried elephant ears
dusted with cinnamon sugar
held hands with future husbands
brought their children to Corn School.

I pull my eyes away from the mural
drop off postcards
the postmistress checks the return address
places me in her world.
This time, I'm the niece of her colleague
the WWII vet turned postman,
I'm the one who just graduated
from college, can you believe it
the one who writes every month

to my grandmother
the nurse who delivered both of her sons,
can you believe it, she smiles
it fades as she remembers
and offers her sympathy.
I thank her, pick up my suitcase,
and continue on my rounds.

I visit the church (Methodist)
where my grandmother was a regular
singing in the choir
Joyful, Joyful, We Adore Thee
and where she brought her tuna casseroles
for after-funeral gatherings.

The door is locked.
I reach into the mailbox, take out the key
and let myself inside
it smells of lemon polish and old books
and faintly, of tuna casserole
I hum under my breath
Joyful, Joyful, We Adore Thee
as I walk to the pastor's office
to leave a final tithe
in memory of my grandmother, and her hometown
gather my suitcase
and leave.

4AM   Toledo

Outside the bus station
the street lights are losing their battle with the darkness.
Inside, the fluorescents buzz and flicker
turning the waiting area
into a morgue.

A bloodless body tilts in its molded plastic seat
eyes closed, then blinking open
not quite focusing on the sleeping shapes on each side
before the eyes close again

near the ticket booth
a hooded figure hunches over a duffle bag
rummaging steadily through its contents
pulling out an item, examining it,
pushing it back into the depths

a snore surfaces
from one corner of the station
and is answered by a chair near the center
they converse without rhythm or purpose
before returning to their own thoughts.

A mop falls over
clattering against linoleum
startling no one,
the sound swallowed by the buzzing lights,

and the sharp exhale of brakes outside.
a loudspeaker shakes itself awake
spewing an indistinct announcement,

an invisible door screeches open
between the bathrooms in the back,
the smell of exhaust and hot metal
wafts through the room,

reanimating the rows of bodies
with yawns and sneezes.

Blurred figures trudge through the gap,
edges sharpening in the harsh light,
a thin dark-skinned woman carries a tear-stained toddler
while dragging a suitcase with a broken wheel,
a colorless teen with a knitted hat
tugs the straps of an overstuffed backpack
a grey-haired man leans heavily on a cane
pausing for breath, then
shuffles across the scarred floor,
past the slouched bodies
in the plastic chairs,
to the front door.

It sticks a little,
then swings open
bringing in the scent of blacktop and burnt rubber
and a faint sound of birdsong.

After The Stroke

When the doctors greet her
she struggles to smile
muscles straining at her lips.
She opens her mouth to stutter hello
but pauses; they are already talking.

Listening
is exhausting.
She has questions to ask
her mouth is dry
her tongue is stone.

Her eyes move from face to face
tracking her name
when it's spoken
each blink slowing her
always one step behind.

Listening
is exhausting.
Too many voices
spiraling to and fro.

As doctors leave the room
she croaks out "wait!"
Unheard in the shuffle of white coats
the door closes behind them.

Listening
is exhausting
she slips away
in moments
when no one is looking.

Homesick

I stand at the window
of my childhood bedroom in Indiana
gaze at bright blue sky
dotted with marshmallow clouds
my mother asks,
"Isn't it nice to be home?"

I squint.
The sunlight I seek
is softer, diffuse
a pearl gray sky
lightly streaked
with feathery wisps
brushing the tips
of mountains
surrounding Seattle.

I clamber
up Queen Anne
slalom down
Capitol Hill
sway on the ferry
taste the salty spray
feel the pull
Mount Rainier imposes
a giant lodestone
capped with snow

My hips ache
when I visit my mother
her house level with the street
I stumble against nothing
on the even sidewalk
unbalanced
this far from home.

Belated

I knew
it was
your birthday
my fingers no longer
hold a pen easily,
but I remember

the cards I sent
filled with words spilling
onto extra pages
torn from notebooks

my pen racing
to keep pace with my thoughts
memories of birthdays past
stories of family news.

Now glancing out the window
as the peonies burst forth
shamelessly preening their assets
lording over the lesser flowers
filling the garden with the fragrance
of birthdays.

The peonies remain,
I am still
at the window
thinking of you.

Memory

She asks me again: Who are you, my dear?
I speak clearly into the phone, and say
I'm Katie, Grandma. I love you, I'm here.

I visit each weekend, since I live near.
Grandma answers the door, dressed up for the day.
She asks me again: who are you, my dear?

We leave her room, destination unclear.
I take her to lunch, she likes the buffet,
I'm Katie, Grandma. I love you, I'm here.

As we walk through the park, we pause to cheer
The toddlers who splash through the water spray.
She asks me again: who are you, my dear?

I sit on the bench, beside her good ear.
We talk and laugh as we watch the kids play.
I'm Katie, Grandma. I love you, I'm here.

I miss my children, she says with a tear.
I kiss her soft cheek, and say it's okay.
She asks me again, Who are you, my dear?
I'm Katie, Grandma. I love you, I'm here.

To The Corner and Back

I am always an adult
in the world of my mother-in-law.
unlike my wife,
who remains a child,
riding her bicycle,
recently freed from training wheels,
all the way to the corner and back.

The memory remains crystal clear
the day she let her daughter bike to the store
four blocks away, out of sight
my Mother-in-law
paints the kitchen ceiling
hangs new wallpaper
watches the sun creep toward the horizon
through the window over the sink.

She never tells me the end of this story
we both know it's happily ever after.
Instead she describes the wallpaper
a repeating pattern of fall bouquets
in harvest gold and green
so deeply etched in her memory
the day her daughter
needed her less
than the day before.

11PM Shopping List

My mother-in-law
is short of breath,
dying by inches
and has a list for me.

This is what I need
it's urgent.
It can't wait. Bring it tonight.

Cough medicine—the strongest you can find.
I need to clear
the ball of phlegm in my throat
I feel it—here—
and I need to bring it up.

Lozenges—the strongest.
Not licorice. Honey or cherry
but strong ones
to reach—here—
and get at that ball stuck in my throat.

Nail clippers—the big ones.
I lost mine, or someone threw them away.

Detergent.
If I must have an aide, I need help with laundry.
not my shirts, I do those myself—
no one else knows the right way.
I put them in the dryer—but not too long
then hang them up
they don't wrinkle.
But maybe she can help
lift the wet clothes to the dryer?

Tissues.
Not the good ones.
I don't need the good ones.

The ones that tear easily
into strips.
I use them
when I finally cough up
that cursed ball of phlegm
it's tiny, a strip is all I need
to wrap it up and throw it away.

Chocolate syrup
for the milk they bring me on the tray,
when I am too tired to walk
the long hallway to the elevator,
and then to the dining room.

Because at age 91, I deserve a treat.

What to Put in the Obituary

Name and birth date, of course,
marital status, children,
but then, the woman at the desk asks
parents' names.
I blink, and hear my mother's voice.

"One year for Christmas"
my mother tells me
"My mother gave me a dime,
and told me to buy gifts for my brothers
and my sisters with it."
There is a whole childhood in that sentence.

She was pulled out of school
starting in grade six
to help at home
to work
to care for the babies
to give her siblings a future.

She stopped attending school after eighth grade
but attended her youngest sister's graduation
and that of her youngest brother as well.

Going through her things,
I found her birth certificate.
Her mother's name is there
and no father is listed.
A mistake, I tell a friend;
no mistake she explains: back then
fathers were not listed
if the parents were not married.

My mother, who never said
a bad thing about anyone
said nothing
about the man her mother married.

The man who was not her father
and never treated her
as a daughter.

I turn my attention back
to the present
to the woman behind the desk.
I ask her to repeat the question.

"I don't remember their names," I tell her.
but even if I did
I will never say them aloud.

Unmothered

"Your mother was such a good friend,"
her neighbor tells me
a hint of Galway threading through her words.

She cries gently
Irish linen handkerchief balled in her hands.
Glancing down, she smooths the fabric gently
watery blue eyes looking past me

remembering how they met
in the book club
getting together for lunch
singing favorite songs
sharing intimate stories

at the end of their lives
hard lived
this day, this hour,
with each other, they were brave
and spoke the unspeakable
aloud.

"We were both unmothered,"
her neighbor explains through tears
stroking the handkerchief
and I imagine
their unraveled threads
shyly brushing each other

their frayed edges
recognizing the pattern
fragile knots connecting
weft and warp
of eldest daughters

tugged from the fabric of family
knotted tightly, pulled askew

ripped in anger
mended with ugly thick stitches
torn again
faded from hard work and tears
stained with untold stories
tossed into a drawer
forgotten for a time.

They find each other in the end
worn thin, nearly translucent
and weave their fragile threads together.

"We were both umothered,"
her neighbor tells me
"and now she is gone."

The Last Jew Standing

The American Dream is standing beside me
frail, but upright, eyes clear
bar mitzvah before 1948
college educated, credentialed, professional.

The American Dream moved his family (yes, also his mother)
to bucolic Queens
spacious apartments looking over gardens
and open to Jews.

The American Dream built a congregation
within walking distance
to daven daily with neighbors
and bring the family for holidays
before differences became schisms,
before children grew up and left
for Westchester, Long Island
Israel.

The American Dream attends community meetings
volunteers at the kosher food pantry
rounds up the minyan
with patience and humor
and the sharing of stories long-known.

Remember Herschel? He always came late
raced through the service
and Lenny, who prayed slowly
how they'd end up at kaddish
right at the same time,

This year
the rabbi died at Passover
the Board President soon after
and two of the neighbors
who always attended daily services
are sick.

but the synagogue will be opened
unlocked by a blue-veined hand that trembles
from a walk that used to feel shorter
the American Dream is still alive.

Dressing the Body

Before the burial
at the veterans cemetery
and the memorial
at the gay bar
I dress his body.

I chose the traditional white yamalkah
even though
he was not traditional.
I chose silk prayer shawl
brought from Berlin
by his father
before the war.

The threads
were ordinary
white
greyed by disuse

and blue
a color
the rabbis say we see
when night ends
and day begins,

and silver
glorious
flashy,
its afterimage
a rainbow
behind the eyelids.

There is so much past
in the past
which thread
do I follow?

Passover 2022

The first time
after lockdown
when we gather
our ragged edges

rub against each other.
We light candles
and name our dead

a father
lost at the beginning
in the panic,
sirens wailing
as he lay silent

a cousin
on a ventilator
nurses holding a cell phone
for family to say goodbye

a neighbor
whose son sits with her body
for days
waiting for an ambulance

We fill our wine cups, mourn
not just the dead
but also the missed opportunities
with our living
never to be regained.

An uncle
isolated from family
believes he will be saved
for he is bathed
in the blood of Christ
and has no need for vaccines

An emergency-room nurse
lacking protective gowns
wrapped in a garbage bag
dunking her gloves
in alcohol
until they fall apart
until she falls apart.

A mother
who survives
in solitary confinement
for her own safety
emerging, bewildered
unable to read the lips
of masked neighbors.

We dedicate a cup of wine
to Dr. Fauci
who has brought us out
of more than one pandemic
we, at the table,
who have visited AIDS wards
held friends in our arms as they died.

It is a tender year
to gather again
to bring all of ourselves
into the room
to let our eyes drift
to the empty chair
and ask

Why is this night different
from all other nights?

ephemera

a creased photograph
stuck inside a paperback
underlined in red on every page.

The paperback
tucked into a cardboard cigar box
filled with postcards
with faded greetings in pencil
hidden in a drawer
next to silk gloves
stained with sweat and rouge.

The gloves
locked in a midcentury dressing table
with a lacquered maple surface
scratched by cocktail rings
prongs missing their stones.
Clip-on earrings seeking their mates
on a table between empty lipstick tubes
and cut glass perfume bottles
reflected in the cloudy mirror.
The mirror
obscured by ticket stubs
held in place by yellowed tape
memories
flaked off with a thumbnail
into dust.

Karen Taylor has written several short stories for anthologies, but this is her first poetry collection. Her work has been included in the Lambda Literary Award winning anthology *First Person Queer: Who We Are So Far* (edited by Richard Labonté and Lawrence Schimel), and in several erotica collections including *The Academy: Tales of the Marketplace* (edited by Laura Antoniou and Karen Taylor), *Best Bisexual Erotica* (edited by Bill Brent and Carol Queen), *Best Transgender Erotica* (edited by Hanne Blank and Raven Kaldera), *Bondage By The Bay* (edited by M. Christian), *Friday the Rabbi Wore Lace* (edited by Karen Tulchinsky), *Leather Ever After* (edited by Sassafras Lowrey), *Leather, Lace & Lust* (edited by M. Christian and Sage Vivant), *Leatherwomen III* (edited by Laura Antoniou), *The Love That Never Dies: Erotic Encounters with the Undead* (edited by M. Christian), *The Mammoth Book of Best New Erotica: Volume 3* (edited by Maxim Jakubowski), *My Lover, My Friend* (edited by Lindsey Elder), *No Other Tribute* (edited by Laura Antoniou), *Pirate Booty* (edited by M. Christian), and *She Who Must Be Obeyed* (edited by D.L. King).

Karen Taylor grew up in Holland, Michigan, the daughter of two English teachers. Her father (T. Kenneth Taylor) was her high school English teacher, and her mother (Nancy Nicodemus) was a professor of English and poetry at Hope College. Karen grew up reading indiscriminately, with home bookshelves filled with American fiction and essays, and weekly visits to her town library. After graduating from Earlham College, Karen moved to Seattle, where she lived for a decade before moving to the East Coast to complete a Masters in Jewish Communal Service at Gratz College.

Karen has spent most of her working life in Older Adult Services as a case manager and program director, focused on helping seniors live independently and at home for as long as possible. She lives in Queens, NY and recently celebrated 25 years with her spouse, author/editor Laura Antoniou.